Bernadette Fitzgerald   Kay Hiatt   Joyce Hil

Oxford Primary English

Book 2

Oxford University Press

Oxford University Press, Walton Street, Oxford OX2 6DP

Oxford New York Toronto
Delhi Bombay Calcutta Madras Karachi
Kuala Lumpur Singapore Hong Kong Tokyo
Nairobi Dar es Salaam Cape Town
Melbourne Auckland Madrid

and associate companies in
Berlin Ibadan

Oxford is a trade mark of Oxford University Press

© Bernadette Fitzgerald, Kay Hiatt and Joyce Hilyer 1992
Published by Oxford University Press 1992
Reprinted 1993

A CIP catalogue record for this book is available from the
British Library.

ISBN 0 19 916557 2

Typeset by Pentacor PLC, High Wycombe, Bucks.

Printed and bound in Great Britain

Contents

Communication

Languages around the world

Aim: *learning about communicating in different languages.*

READ In groups of four, look at these words. How many of these can you read and say?

READ
TALK

They all mean 'welcome'.

Have you noticed the different alphabets and scripts here?

If you can say 'welcome', or 'hello', in another language, share it with the group.

Below are the titles of four different tales from around the world. Make up a group story using one of these titles. Then each group can tell their story to the rest of the class.

AN ARABIAN TALE

الرّاعِي

The shepherd

AN INDIAN TALE

सूर्य ग्रहण

The eclipse of the sun

A CELTIC TALE

Ar Luvet

Flash of lightning

A CHINESE TALE

絲 鬍 子

The silken beard

Publish your story for the class library. Remember to copy the title in English *and* in the other script.

Communication

Languages around us

**Aim: learning more about other languages—
in the world, in the street, in your school.**

READ

Languages in the world

In 1987, this number of people spoke these languages at home:

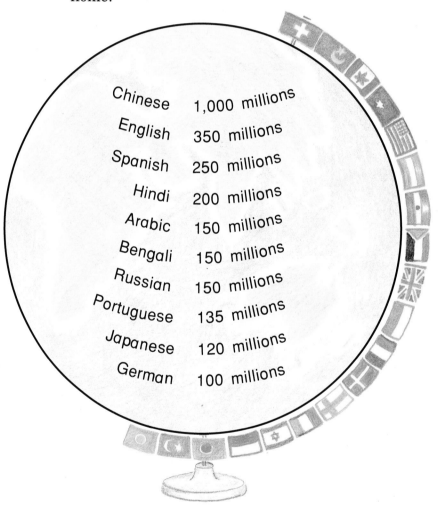

Chinese	1,000 millions
English	350 millions
Spanish	250 millions
Hindi	200 millions
Arabic	150 millions
Bengali	150 millions
Russian	150 millions
Portuguese	135 millions
Japanese	120 millions
German	100 millions

TALK

WRITE

Did anything about this list surprise you? Why do you think English is spoken by so many people?

On your own, look again at the list and put this information into a graph.

READ
TALK

Languages in the street

How many different languages can you see on the restaurant signs below?

Next time you go shopping, make a list of the different languages you see around you to share with the rest of the class.

READ

Languages in your school

This is part of a language survey carried out by some children in their class.

Name	Language(s) spoken	A little	A lot
Ming-Yan	Cantonese English		✓ ✓
Sharon	Polish English	✓	✓
Jonathon	English		✓

TALK
WRITE

- Make your own chart like the one above.
- Ask the children in your class which languages they speak.
- Fill in their answers on your chart.
- Put your information into a bar graph.

Communication

Getting on with one another

Aim: learning about ways of greeting and making friends.

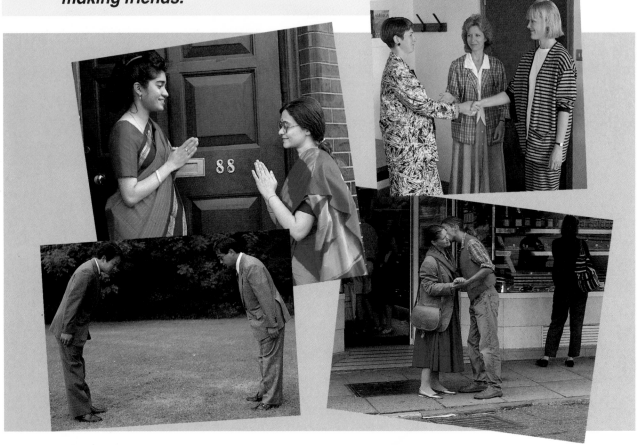

READ
TALK
ACT

In pairs, talk about what these people are doing. Why is it important to do these things? What do you think they might be saying to each other?

Now make up a new way to greet a friend. Practise it, and then show the rest of your class.

READ
WRITE
DRAW

Read these two poems out loud to your partner. Talk about them together.

Write out your favourite one in your best handwriting.

Draw pictures to go with it.

Let's Talk

Lips are for speaking
And smiling too.
Tongues are for saying
How do you do?

Hands are for waving
To people on the street
And hearts are for loving
Everyone we meet.

Ask the person on your left
If he would be your friend
Then turn to your right
And do the same again.

Telcine Turner

How to Say Hello

Kiss a baby
Pat a dog
Stroke a kitten
Scratch a hog
Curtsey to a queen
Or bow,
Chase a chicken,
Call a cow;
If any other
Thing should greet you
Say 'How do you do?
I'm pleased to meet you.'
(Unless you think
It wants to eat you.)

Dennis Doyle

WRITE

On your own, write a list of instructions on how to make and keep friends, like the one we've started below.

How to make and keep friends
1. Smile to begin with.
2. Greet each other in some way.
3. . . . .
4. . . . .

Story

Setting

Aim: learning about where stories happen.

Writers of stories have to decide:

* what the story is going to be about
* who the characters are going to be
* **where the story will happen**

A

On the other side of the water there stood a strong, stone castle with great round towers at each end. In the middle, a massive wooden door guarded the entrance to the fortress.

TALK
WRITE

These are two different settings for stories. In pairs, talk about how they are different.

On a piece of paper make two columns. In the first column write Picture A. In the second column write Picture B. Then look carefully at the two pictures. Compare the two pictures, and write down the differences between them.

Picture A	Picture B
On the ground	In the sky

B

There hanging in the sky above him was the castle of the little sister of the sun. Beautiful it was, made of cloud, and hanging in the sky as if it were built of red roses.

From *Prince Ivan, the Witch Baby and the Little Sister of the Sun.*

DRAW

On your own, think of a setting for a story you would like to write, and draw or paint a picture of it. It could be in a town, in the country, at the seaside, on a different planet, under water, in a desert, in a jungle . . .

- First, decide what you are going to put in your picture. Close your eyes and try to see it.
- Next, write a list of everything you want to include.
- When you finish your picture, keep it in a safe place. You will need it later on.

Story

Word paintings

Aim: learning about how writers describe setting in a story.

Good writers paint pictures with words.

> READ

These are some of the ways well-known writers have described settings in their stories. They have started their stories with a description of a place. Later in their stories the settings can change.

In a small group, take it in turns to read the passages out loud. As you listen, try to imagine what the places look like.

Once upon a time there was a wood-mouse, and her name was Mrs Tittlemouse. She lived in a bank under a hedge. Such a funny house! There were yards and yards of sandy passages, leading to storerooms and nut-cellars and seed-cellars, all amongst the roots of the hedge. There was a kitchen, a parlour, a pantry, and a larder. Also, there was Mrs Tittlemouse's bedroom, where she slept in a little box bed!

From *The Tale of Mrs Tittlemouse* by Beatrix Potter

Every afternoon, as they were coming from school, the children used to go to play in the Giant's garden.

It was a lovely garden, with soft green grass. Here and there over the grass stood beautiful flowers like stars, and there were twelve peach-trees that in spring-time broke out into delicate blossoms of pink and pearl, and in the autumn bore rich fruit. The birds sat on the trees and sang so sweetly that the children used to stop their games in order to listen to them.

From *The Selfish Giant* by Oscar Wilde

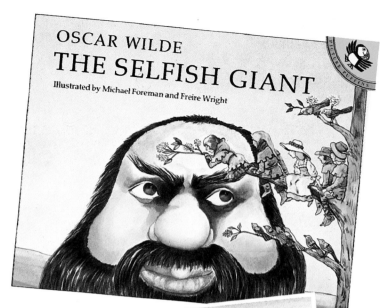

All through the warm summer night, the people of Ayodha, a kingdom in ancient India, worked to prepare their city for the morrow's celebrations, the coronation of their beloved Prince Rama. They hung gay lanterns from balconies and tree tops, and adorned the white temples of the city with banners and bamboo archways. They burned fragrant incense and strewed flowers upon all sides – roses, jasmine and marigolds. The people were in great good humour; there was not one who did not look forward to the celebrations, for Rama and his young wife, Sita, were the idols of the people's hearts.

From *The Adventures of Rama and Sita* by Ruskin Bond

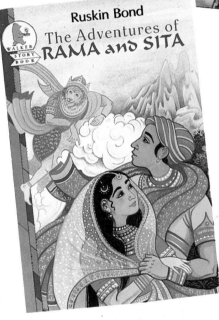

WRITE

When you have heard them all, choose the setting which you like best.

On your own, make a list of the words which help to create the setting. Here is one started for you:

The Selfish Giant
lovely garden
soft green grass

Notice that the authors introduce characters while they are describing the settings.

Now look again at the picture that you have already made and write about it as the setting for what will happen in your story.

Story

Becoming a story writer

READ

Samantha wanted to write a story of her own so she planned it like this. She asked herself these questions.

What type of story will it be?
Who will be in the story?
Where will the story take place?
When will the story happen?
What will happen in the story?
What shall I call it?

She then chose the ingredients for her story carefully.

In a small group, look at the range she had to choose from. Maybe you can think of others.

14

TALK

Still in your small group, choose a story you all know well.

Decide which ingredients have been used to write this story. You will find most of them already on the shelves. Are there any others?

Story

Samantha's story

Aim: learning how to write a story.

READ ▷

Samantha mixed her ingredients like this:

Recipe for a Story

Ingredients:

Type of story: Adventure

Characters: Who will be in the story? What will they be like?

A little girl called Susie ⟶ she is kind
Her pet fish called Goldie ⟶ who can talk like humans
The King of the Underwater people → who is friendly and kind

Setting: Where will the story take place?

1. Susie's bedroom / 2. Under the sea

Time: When will the story take place?

In the present / at night

Ideas for the plot: What will happen in the story?

Beginning: Susie is asleep and she hears her fish talk.

Middle: Susie goes to the underwater Kingdom with her fish and is invited to a feast.

End: Her fish takes her back home again.

Story title: What shall I call it?

The Underwater Kingdom

Method: Follow the Writing Pathway.

Result: A story to share with friends.

READ

Here is part of Samantha's story after she had revised and edited it. We have marked it to show you how the ideas from her story planner appear in her story. Notice how she has written it in paragraphs.

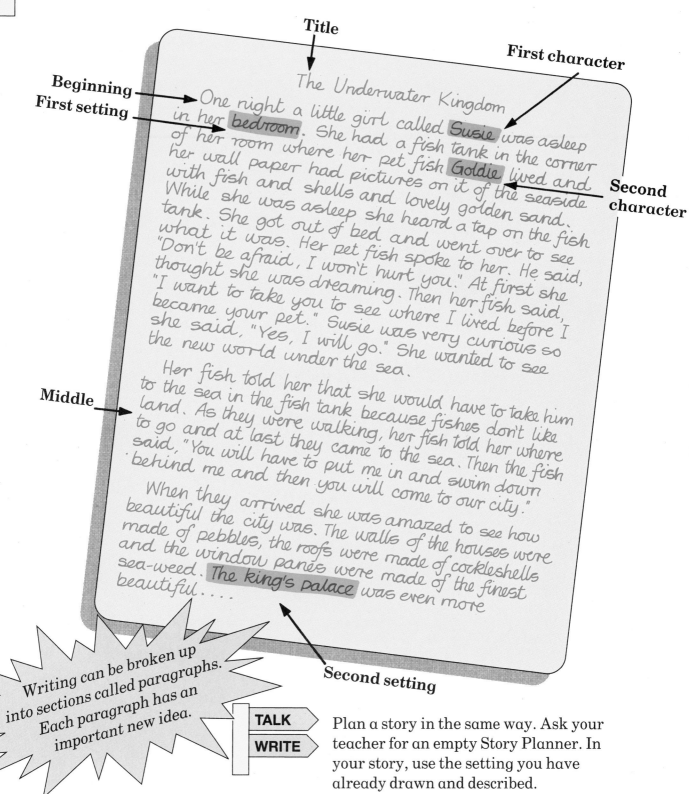

Title

First character

Second character

Beginning
First setting

Middle

Second setting

The Underwater Kingdom

One night a little girl called Susie was asleep in her bedroom. She had a fish tank in the corner of her room where her pet fish Goldie lived and her wall paper had pictures on it of the seaside with fish and shells and lovely golden sand. While she was asleep she heard a tap on the fish tank. She got out of bed and went over to see what it was. Her pet fish spoke to her. He said, "Don't be afraid, I won't hurt you." At first she thought she was dreaming. Then her fish said, "I want to take you to see where I lived before I became your pet." Susie was very curious so she said, "Yes, I will go." She wanted to see the new world under the sea.

Her fish told her that she would have to take him to the sea in the fish tank because fishes don't like land. As they were walking, her fish told her where to go and at last they came to the sea. Then the fish said, "You will have to put me in and swim down behind me and then you will come to our city."

When they arrived she was amazed to see how beautiful the city was. The walls of the houses were made of pebbles, the roofs were made of cockleshells and the window panes were made of the finest sea-weed. The king's palace was even more beautiful. . . .

Writing can be broken up into sections called paragraphs. Each paragraph has an important new idea.

TALK
WRITE

Plan a story in the same way. Ask your teacher for an empty Story Planner. In your story, use the setting you have already drawn and described.

17

Thinking about writing

What and why?

> **Aim:** *learning about reasons for writing and what we write.*

READ
TALK
WRITE

In a small group, on a large sheet of paper, brainstorm the reasons why we need to be able to write. This is a brainstorm which Susie and Campbell started:

Why do we need to write?

Reasons

to invite friends to a party

to remember what to buy in the supermarket

A reason for writing is called a **purpose.**

Now think of all the writing which *you* have done over the last twenty-four hours. On your own, fill it in on a chart like the one which Susie has done below:

My writing over the last 24 hours

When I wrote it...	What I wrote...
Before school... at home	Wrote a birthday card to a friend
Morning school...	Filled in my story planner Wrote notes about Science experiment we did
Afternoon school...	Wrote about my favourite food graph. Wrote letter for information about my food topic
After school at home	Finished my crossword Wrote in my diary

You will need your chart to help you when you turn over.

TALK ▷

With a partner, talk about why you think that Susie needed to do all of this writing.

Now talk about why you needed to do your writing.

Thinking about writing

Who reads it?

Aim: learning about who reads our writing.

Susie thought about the different people who read her writing. Look at the pictures below and talk about who they were. Now make a list of all the readers.

"I read my diary last night."

"My friend read my story planner."

"My sister read the birthday card I sent her."

A person who reads your writing is called the **audience**.

"The managing director read my letter asking for an information pack and a poster."

"My teacher read my science notes."

"My dad read the crossword I had finished."

READ
WRITE

Look again at your chart, 'My writing over the last 24 hours'. Think about *who* reads your writing. Make a list using the heading, 'Audiences For My Writing'.

21

Thinking about writing

What we write

Aim: learning about different types of writing.

READ
TALK
WRITE

With a partner, read and talk about the different types of writing you can see on the noticeboard. Now make a list of the different types.

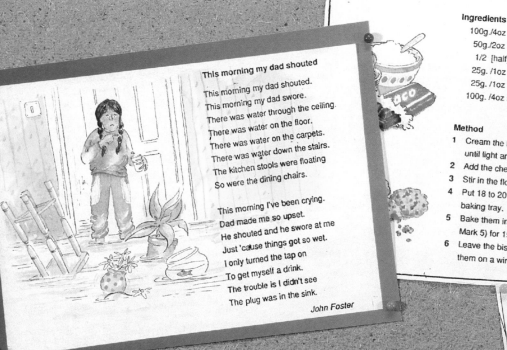

This morning my dad shouted

This morning my dad shouted.
This morning my dad swore.
There was water through the ceiling.
There was water on the floor.
There was water on the carpets.
There was water down the stairs.
The kitchen stools were floating
So were the dining chairs.

This morning I've been crying.
Dad made me so upset.
He shouted and he swore at me
Just 'cause things got so wet.
I only turned the tap on
To get myself a drink.
The trouble is I didn't see
The plug was in the sink.

John Foster

te cherry cookies

Ingredients

100g./4oz butter
50g./2oz caster sugar
1/2 [half] teaspoon vanilla essence
25g. /1oz finely chopped glacé cherries
25g. /1oz finely chopped plain chocolate
100g. /4oz sifted plain flour

Method

1 Cream the butter with the sugar and the vanilla essence until light and fluffy.
2 Add the cherries and the chocolate.
3 Stir in the flour.
4 Put 18 to 20 teaspoons of the mixture, well apart, on the baking tray.
5 Bake them in a moderately hot oven (190°C/375°F or Gas Mark 5) for 15 to 20 minutes.
6 Leave the biscuits on the trays for 1 to 2 minutes, then put them on a wire rack to cool.

INDEX

aerosol spray 22
animal 12
Antarctica 4,10,11,12,23
Arctic 4,10,11,12,22
Atlantic Ocean 10
atmosphere 22,23

blubber 14

carnivore 14
colony 12
crop 16

fish 12,13
floating ice 6
fur 12,14,16

glacier 4
greenhouse effect 23
Greenland 10,14

helicopter 20

ice crystals 6
ice rivers 4
ice sheet 4,10
icebergs 4,6,8,11,12,21
          tabular 4,8,11
icebreaker 18
International Ice Patrol 10

krill 13

North Pole 4,12

oil 22
oil rig 22
ozone

peng
polar
polar
poll
pup

sc
sc
se
s

To t

Entr

TALK
WRITE

What different types of writing have you done in class? Think and talk about them.

Types of Writing

Ali,

...e to my birthday party
3rd May at 4pm
...e 6 Grove Road,
...esthaven.
...om Jason

rsvp

Mother Hubbard, she went to the cupboard
...etch her poor dog a bone,
...when she got there, the cupboard was bare,
...so the poor dog had none.

Class 4,
Parkside Primary School,
Glasgow
4th November, 1992.

Dear Mohammed,
　　　　In our class
we've been making safety posters
for Bonfire Night.
　　I'm going to a Fireworks'
Party. Are you going to one?
Tell me if you are.

　　　　Love from,
　　　　Simon

Why do we need to write?

Reasons

to invite friends to a party

to remember what to buy in the supermarket

Knock-knock.
Who's there?
Ivor.
Ivor who?
Ivor you open the door or
I'll climb through the window.

The Underwater Kingdom

One night a little girl called Susie was asleep in her bedroom. She had a fish tank in the corner of her room where her pet fish Goldie lived and her wall paper had pictures on it of the seaside with fish and shells and lovely golden sand. While she was asleep she heard a tap on the fish tank. She got out of bed and went over to see what it was. Her pet fish spoke to her. He said, "Don't be afraid, I won't hurt you." At first she thought she was dreaming. Then her fish said, "I want to take you to see where I lived before I became your pet." Susie was very curious so she said, "Yes, I will go." She wanted to see the new world under the sea.

Her fish told her that she would have to take him to the sea in the fish tank because fishes don't like land. As they were walking, her fish told her where to go and at last they came to the sea. Then the fish said, "You will have to put me in and swim down behind me and then you will come to our city."

When they arrived she was amazed to see how beautiful the city was. The walls of the houses were made of pebbles, the roofs were made of cockleshells and the window panes were made of the finest sea-weed. The king's palace was even more beautiful....

End of term Concert

...eld in: Wood Green Primary School
　　on: July 20th
　　at: 6.30 p.m.

...e charge: £1 adults
　　　　50p children and senior citizens

Refreshments available!

Writing to instruct

Recipe

Aim: learning about recipes.

Instructions should be clear and in the right order.

> **READ**

Amit and Lucy were making some biscuits with their teacher to sell at their school fete. This is the recipe they used. Read it together in your small group.

Chocolate Cherry Cookies

Ingredients

- 100g/4oz butter
- 50g/2oz caster sugar
- ½ teaspoon vanilla essence
- 25g/1oz finely chopped glacé cherries
- 25g/1oz finely chopped plain chocolate
- 100g/4oz sifted plain flour

What you need

What to do

Method

1 Cream the butter with the sugar and the vanilla essence until light and fluffy.
2 Add the cherries and the chocolate.
3 Stir in the flour.
4 Put 18 to 20 teaspoons of the mixture, well apart, on the baking tray.
5 Bake them in a moderately hot oven (190°C/375°F or Gas Mark 5) for 15 to 20 minutes.
6 Leave the biscuits on the trays for 1 to 2 minutes, then put them on a wire rack to cool.

These instructions begin with a verb. 'Cream', 'add', 'stir' are all verbs.

Lucy likes the peanut biscuits her grandmother bakes. She wrote and asked for the recipe so that she could take it to school. This is what her grandmother said in her letter.

Dear Lucy,

It was lovely getting your letter. I am so pleased that you like my peanut biscuits and want to make them to sell at your school fête.

This is what you'll need to do. First weigh out 100g. of butter and 50g. of caster sugar and put these into a mixing bowl. Then get a wooden spoon and beat them together until the mixture is light and fluffy. Now you'll have to weigh 150g. of plain flour and stir this into the mixture until you have a stiff dough. Take care not to get the flour all over the place! Roll out the dough evenly until it is 6mm (¼ in.) thick. Make sure though that you first sprinkle flour on the table and onto your rolling pin. Next you'll need to get a round cutter and cut out your biscuits. I think this will make about 20. Put them onto a greased baking tray and brush the tops with milk and then sprinkle on some chopped nuts – about 50g. of peanuts will be enough. Bake them in a moderate oven – about 180°C / 350°F or Gas Mark 4 for about 12 minutes. Then leave them to cool for a minute or so before you lift them carefully onto a wire rack to cool properly.

I hope they turn out all right and you sell them all. Let me know.

Love,
Gran.

WRITE

Lucy only wants the recipe to take to school. Can you help her by writing it out clearly?

- First list the ingredients. Remember to give the correct amounts.
- Then write the method. The recipe on page 24 shows you how to set it out.

Have you got a favourite recipe?

Writing to instruct

A recipe with a difference!

 READ In a small group, one of you read this recipe out loud.

Recipe for Making Parents Shout

You will need:

A puddle

Some soil

A small spade
(if not, hands will do)

A younger brother or sister

Method:

1 Wait until rain stops.

2 Ask to play outside (best to ask 20 or 30 times).

3 Outside, find a medium size puddle.

4

Get soil from garden and add to puddle.
Mix well.
Repeat until puddle is thick,
black and sticky.

5

Walk through puddle (three or four times).
Let younger brother or sister stand
in puddle.

6

Then

Walk into house (best if everyone else
is upstairs).

7

Run through every room shouting the
words, 'Come and look at this'.
This recipe always makes adults shout
but works best if your house has pale
coloured carpets.

Martyn Wiley

 TALK

Why do you think this piece
of writing is called a recipe?

What is the difference
between this recipe and the
one on page 24?

 WRITE

Work on your own or with a
partner and write a recipe
like the one above. It can be
to make someone happy
instead of cross.

Choose a title like 'Recipe
for Making a Parent Happy'
or 'Recipe for Making My
Teacher Happy'.

About ourselves

Our baby talk

READ
TALK

In small groups, look at these pictures of babies. Say what you think the baby and adult in each picture might be saying.

TALK
WRITE
DRAW

First words

Talk about the first words which your brothers, sisters, or cousins said when they were babies.

Write a list of their first words.

When you go home, ask your family:

- What were the first words you said as a baby?
- How old were you when you said them?

Add these words to your group list of first words.

Draw a picture of you as a baby or bring in a baby photograph from home. Stick it on a piece of paper. Write your first words in a speech bubble by the picture.

TALK
ACT
WRITE

Do you talk differently when you talk to a baby?

Which words do you use?

In pairs, act out talking to a baby. Take it in turns to be the baby in the following situations:

- a baby crying in a high chair
- a baby playing with toys
- a baby gurgling in a pram.

After you have acted them out, choose the situation which you enjoyed most. Write it out as a playscript. Set it out like this:

    Me: Oh, what's the matter then, baby kinsy winsy?
Baby: Wah! Wah! Wail!

About ourselves

George speaks

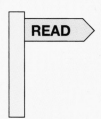

READn

Can you imagine how funny it would be if babies could
* understand everything we say to them
* talk back to us in grown-up language?

In the following story, Laura discovers that her four-week-old baby brother, George, is no ordinary baby.

Read on to discover how George is extraordinary!

'Don't wake George up, will you?' her mother had said. 'I'll be in the kitchen if you want me.'

'I won't wake you,' Laura said to the sleeping baby. 'And I don't want to sound rude. But I must tell you something. You look just like a little pig.'

And that was when it happened.

The baby opened his eyes and stared straight at her. 'Pig yourself,' he said.

Laura gasped. A shiver ran up her spine and her toes tingled.

'What did you say?' she whispered.

'I said, "Pig yourself",' said George, 'You're not deaf, are you?'

'No,' said Laura. 'No, it's just that I didn't expect you to say anything.'

'Why not?'

'Well, babies don't say proper words. They only make noises, like Goo-goo or Blur-blur or Wah.'

'Is that a fact?' said the baby.

'Yes,' said Laura. 'It is. However can you talk like that when you're only four weeks old? It's amazing! I must run and tell Mum.'

She turned to dash out of the room.
'Laura!' said the baby sharply.
Laura turned back.
'Yes, George?' she said.
The baby looked at her very severely, his forehead creased into a little frown.
'On no account are you to tell our mother,' he said. 'Or anyone else for that matter. This is a secret between you and me. Do you understand?'
'Yes, George,' said Laura.

'I've been waiting for some time now,' said George, 'to speak to you on your own. This is the first proper chance I've had, what with feeding and bathing and nappy-changing and people coming to see me all the time. And talk about making noises – it's all some of them do. They bend over me with silly grins on their faces, and then they come out with a load of rubbish. "Who's booful den?" "Who's a gorgeous Georgeous Porgeous?" "Diddums wassums Granny's ickle treasure?" It's an insult to the English language.'

'But George,' said Laura, 'how do you know the English language?'
'Well, I'm English, aren't I?'
'Yes, but how did you learn it?'
'Same way as you, I imagine. Listening to grown-ups talking. I wasn't born yesterday, you know.'

If you enjoyed this and want to read about what happens in the rest of the story, you will find it in a book called *George Speaks* by Dick King-Smith.

About ourselves

Our early memories

Aim: learning about how writers describe their early memories.

READ ▷ Read what these three authors have chosen to write about when they were young.

I woke up when the bomb came through the roof. It came through at an angle, overflew my bed by inches, bounced up over my mother's bed, hit the mirror, dropped into the grate and exploded up the chimney. It was an incendiary. A fire-bomb.

Michael Foreman from War Boy – A Country Childhood

Growing Up

When I was one, I tended to cry,
and spat out my dummy in my mum's eye.

When I was two, I could walk and talk,
and could eat with a knife, spoon and fork.

When I was three, I could run and jump,
but once I fell and received a bump.

When I was four, I went to school,
but didn't like it, the teachers were cruel.

When I was five, I was making things,
and we all made crowns to look like kings.

When I was six, I could climb and play war,
and we would snipe, crawling on the floor.

Now that I'm older, I've just reached seven,
I look at Andrew and wish I was eleven.

Robert

I have a very firm earliest memory. I, the first born, was three and a half and my mother was expecting another child. I was constantly asking God to send *me* a new brother or sister. The 'me' was important because I loved receiving parcels and presents that *I* could open. I was outraged when the baby arrived, because all the attention shifted from me to this small red-faced thing in a cot. It was a great disappointment to me. I had been praying for this moment; and now here was this 'thing', wailing and wailing, and everybody was saying how beautiful it was. 'Honestly,' I said, 'I would have preferred a rabbit!' And I would have preferred a rabbit at that time because although my school pals had brothers and sisters I had wanted a rabbit for ages. For the next three years I wanted to send my sister back. When I think of the great friendship I have with her now I cringe at the thought of wanting to exchange her for a rabbit when I was three and a half years old.

Maeve Binchy
from *A Portrait of the Artist as a Young Girl*

 WRITE

Choose one of your own early memories to write about. It can be written either

• in prose like Michael Foreman and Maeve Binchy did,
    or
• as a poem, like Robert did.

You can add your writing to your class book on 'Ourselves'.

About ourselves

Our early reading

> **Aim:** *learning about where and what we used to read.*

READD
TALK

In a small group, talk about where the children are reading in the pictures above. Do you remember where you used to enjoy stories?

Now talk about and list some of the books you used to read. Talk about why you liked them.

Now draw and fill in a chart like the one opposite.

34

Name of book	Where it was read	Who read it with you
My Naughty Little Sister Goes Fishing	On the settee	My Mum

Ask at home if you can bring in some of your first books.
You will need them for the next pages.

About ourselves

Our first favourites

Aim: talking about the books we used to enjoy.

TALK

In a small group, talk about the cover of this book. It is a favourite book for young children.

- What is the title?
- Who are the author and the illustrator?
- What is in the picture?

Do you think a little child would like this cover? Say why.

Now talk about the covers of the books you have brought in. Use the questions above to help you.

READ

In a small group, read the opening page of *My Naughty Little Sister Goes Fishing*.

A long time ago, when I was a little girl, I had a sister who was very much younger than me. Although my sister was often naughty, most of the naughty things she did were so funny that no one was cross with her for very long and she made a lot of friends.

Here is a story about one of my sister's adventures. It is called My Naughty Little Sister Goes Fishing.

One day, when I was a little girl, and my sister was a very little girl, some children came to our house and asked my mother if I could go fishing with them.

They had jam-jars with string on them, and fishing-nets and sandwiches and lemonade.

READ >
TALK >

Talk about

- how the author begins the story
- what she says about the characters
- what you can see in the illustration
- what you think about how Shirley Hughes has drawn the illustrations
- the size of the print
- how the pages are laid out.

Now take it in turns to read aloud one of the books you have brought in. Do you still like it?

About ourselves

Write your own

Aim: learning how to write a book for young children.

Remember the Writing Pathway.

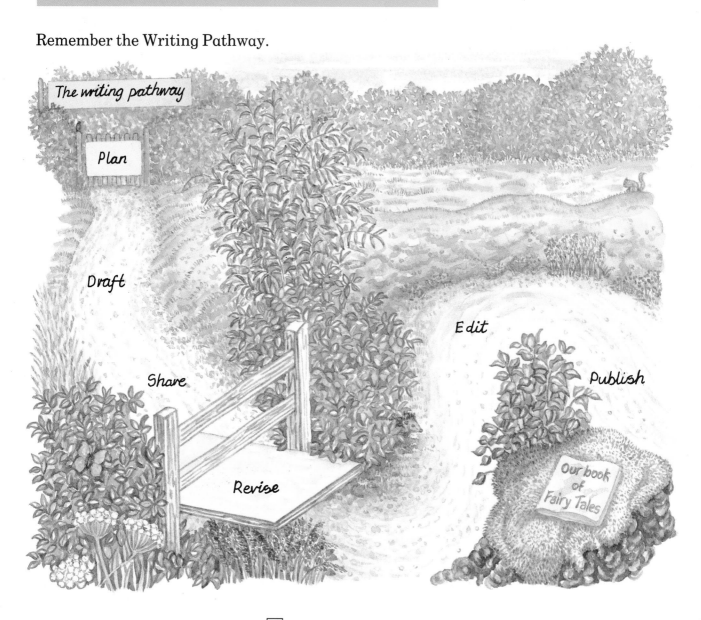

The writing pathway

Plan

Draft

Share

Revise

Edit

Publish

Our book of Fairy Tales

READ ▷
WRITE ▷

You have talked about the stories *you* used to enjoy – now you are going to write and publish a book for younger children to read and enjoy.

Start with a Story Planner (see pages 16 and 17).

Publishing your book

Think carefully about

- who is going to read it
- the size of your book
- the shape of your book
- the title
- the cover
- the illustrations.

Will they be hand-written, word processed, or typed?

Which size print or writing will you use?

How much writing will you put on each page?

Will the illustrations go on the same pages as the writing?

Will the book contain 'pop-up' or moveable pictures?

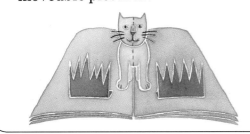

Anything else?

Which type and colour of paper or card will you use?

When your book is finished, share it with a younger child.

Finding information

The fact-finding trail

Aim: learning how to get information by following the fact-finding trail.

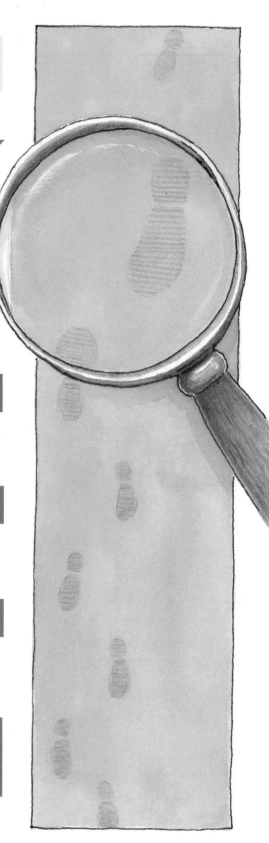

This way for the fact-finding trail.

Start here

What do I already know?

What more do I want to know?

How do I get the information?

What shall I do with the information?

This term's topic is food

In pairs, the class was asked to find out more about their favourite foods, to go in a class 'Food' book for the library. Here are some of their favourites:

Leroy and Helen loved baked beans and started on the fact-finding trail with a brainstorm.

What do I already know?

What more do I want to know?

Leroy and Helen wanted to know:

- Where do baked beans come from?
- How are they baked?

They wrote these questions down on a clipboard.

Finding information

Who to ask, where to look

How do I get the information?

READ

By asking people.

Leroy and Helen asked their teacher.

They asked their friends.

By using the library.

They looked at the video section.

They checked the data-bases.

They looked through magazines.

They looked through their booklet on where to find books in the library. It was called a subject index.

Here are two pages from their 'where to look' subject index booklet.

Libraries outside school have books like these to help you.

In the subject index booklet, subjects are arranged alphabetically, like in a dictionary.

Each subject has a number. The number will help you to find the book that you want on the shelf of the library.

Fabrics		677
Factories		338
Fairs		394 & 791
Fairy tales		398
Families		301
Famine		301 & 641
Farming		630
Fencing		796
Ferns		587
Festivals		394
Films		791
Finland	*geography*	914.8
	history	948
Fire		536

Fire service		614
First aid		614
Fishes		597
Fishing		799
Fishing industry		639
Flags		929
Flower arranging		745
Flowers	*garden*	635
	wild	582
Folklore		398
Food		641
Food manufacture		664
Football		796

TALK

Which were the numbers for food and food manufacture?
If they had wanted to find information on factories or farming, which numbers would they have looked under?

Finding information

Books which help

How do I get the information?

These are the books that Leroy and Helen found under the food number. Which one do you think they looked at first?

Yes, they chose *Beans* by Terry Jennings.

This is how they got the information they wanted.

They used the contents page from the beginning of the book.

Beans

Terry Jennings
Photographs by Ed Barber

Contents

A & C Black · London

44

They used the index page from the end of the book.

Both these pages helped them to find answers to their questions. Which pages did they turn to?

Can you remember what their questions were? Look back to page 41 to check if you were right.

Index

(Numbers in bold type are pages which show activities.)

Finding information

The end of the trail

How do I get the information?

Baked beans: the story

Canned baked beans have been around since 1875. They were first made in America. Have you ever wondered how today's baked beans are made?

Baked beans are really haricot beans, grown in North America and Canada. They are dried, and shipped to Britain in sacks.

In the baked beans factory, a worker slits open the sacks and tips the beans down a big funnel. Machines then sort them by size and colour. Any that are too small or dark end up in buckets, and will be sold as animal food.

Beans of the right size and colour are passed through tanks and pipes that wash them and partly cook them. They become softer.

16

READ

Together Leroy and Helen looked at the pictures and read the pages. Then they looked again at the questions they had written down.

- Where do baked beans come from?
- How are they baked?

Read these pages to find out the answers to their questions.

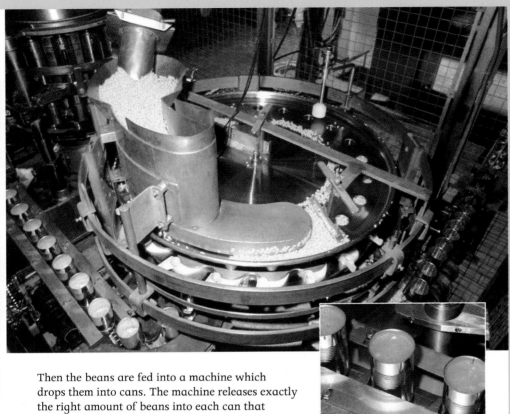

Then the beans are fed into a machine which drops them into cans. The machine releases exactly the right amount of beans into each can that comes along.

Another machine adds the tomato sauce, and then the cans have their lids sealed on. Finally, they are heated to 130°C, to kill any bacteria or fungi which might make the beans go bad. A machine sticks on the labels, and a factory worker gives the cans one last check. Then they're ready to be delivered to shops and supermarkets.

What shall I do with the information?

They used the information from

- their brainstorm
- their friends
- their teacher
- this information book

to write two pages for their class book on 'Food'.

Acknowledgements

The publishers would like to thank the following for permission to reproduce copyright material:

Sonia Allison, from *The Dairy Book of Home Cookery* (1968), by permission of the Milk Marketing Board; **Maeve Binchy**, from John Quinn (Ed.), *A Portrait of the Artist as a Young Girl*, by permission of the publishers, Methuen London; **Ruskin Bond**, from *The Adventures of Rama and Sita*, illustrated by Valerie Littlewood, text © Ruskin Bond 1987, illustrations © Valerie Littlewood 1987, published in the U. K. by Walker Books Ltd., by permission of the publishers; **Suzanne Bukiet**, from *Scripts of the World*, by permission of the publishers, Mantra Publishing Ltd; **Chris Deshpande**, from *Finger Foods* (A. & C. Black, 1986), and **Annabelle Dixon**, from *Milk*, photographed by Chris Fairclough, (A. & C. Black, 1987) both by permission of the publishers; **Dorothy Edwards** and **Shirley Hughes** (illustrator), from *My Naughty Little Sister Goes Fishing*, by permission of the publishers, Methuen Children's Books; **Michael Foreman**, from *War Boy* (Pavilion Books, 1989) by permission of the publishers; **Terry Jennings**, from *Beans*, photographed by Ed Barber, illustrated by Katherine Greenwood (A. & C. Black, 1990), by permission of the publishers; **Dick King-Smith**, from *George Speaks*, illustrated by Judy Brown (Viking, 1988), text © Dick King-Smith 1988, illustrations © Judy Brown 1988, by permission of A. P. Watt Ltd., and Penguin Books Ltd; **David Marshall**, from *Food* (1987), © Macdonald and Co. (Publishers) Ltd. 1987, by permission of Simon & Schuster Young Books, Hemel Hempstead, U.K.; **Beatrix Potter**, from *The Tale of Mrs Tittlemouse*, © Frederick Warne & Co., 1910, 1987, by permission of Frederick Warne & Co.; **Arthur Ransome**, from *Old Peter's Russian Tales* (Cape, 1984) by permission of the Random Century Group; **Telcine Turner**, from *Song of the Surreys*, by permission of the publishers, Macmillan Education Ltd., **Oscar Wilde**, from *The Selfish Giant*, illustrated by Michael Foreman and Freire Wright, first published by Kaye & Ward Ltd., by permission of William Heinemann Ltd.; and **Martyn Wiley**, 'Recipe for Making Parents Shout', first published here, © Martyn Wiley 1992, by permission of the author.

We are also grateful to Bill Boyle for the poem by **Robert** from *What's in a Poem* edited by Bill Boyle (Collins Educational); Moonlight Publishing Ltd. for the front cover of *Fruit*, illustrated by P. M. Valat, created by Gallimard Jeunesse and Pascale de Bourgoing © 1989 by Editions Gallimard, translated by Sarah Matthews, English text © 1990 by Moonlight Publishing Ltd.; Wayland (Publishers) Ltd. for the front covers of *Apples* and *Cheese*; and the ZEFA (UK) agency for the front cover of *Growing Food* (Simon & Schuster Young Books, 1991).

'The Underwater Kingdom' was written by Samantha Adams of Fonthill Junior School, Avon.

Although every effort has been made to trace and contact copyright holders before publication, this has not been possible in some cases. We apologize for any infringement of copyright and will be pleased to rectify any omissions at the earliest opportunity.

Photographs: City of Edinburgh District Council p.23 (top right); Ander McIntyre pp. 7, 8; Collections/Roy Stedall Humphryes p. 10.

The illustrations are by: Ian Beck p. 23 (bottom left); Bucket pp. 22 (right), 24/25, 40, 41; Tony Chance p. 28; Paul Dowling p. 23 (top left, bottom right); Jane Gedye p. 22 (left); Kimmie McHarrie p. 9; Diana Mayo, p. 11; Isobel Morgan Giles pp. 4–5, 6, 33; Claire Pound pp. 20–21, 34–35; Pam Stephens p. 38; Julie Tolliday pp. 18, 29, 33 (bottom), 39; Renee Williams pp. 14–15, 26–27, 42.

The handwriting on pp. 7, 9, 10, 13, 16, 17, 18, 19, 23, 25, 35, and 41 is by Elitta Fell.

Cover illustration is by Peter Joyce.